no
quiz

THE ALLISONS

RACE CAR LEGENDS

COLLECTOR'S EDITION

A.J. Foyt

The Allisons

Dale Earnhardt Jr.

Danica Patrick

Famous Finishes

Famous Tracks

The Jarretts

Jeff Burton

Jeff Gordon

Jimmie Johnson

Kenny Irwin Jr.

The Labonte Brothers

Lowriders

Mario Andretti

Mark Martin

Monster Trucks & Tractors

Motorcycles

The Need for Speed

Off-Road Racing

The Pit Crew

Rockcrawling

Rusty Wallace

Stunt Driving

Tony Stewart

The Unsers

THE ALLISONS

Ann Parr

CHELSEA HOUSE
PUBLISHERS
An imprint of Infobase Publishing

The Allisons

© 2007 by Infobase Publishing

Chelsea House
An imprint of Infobase Publishing
132 West 31st Street
New York NY 10001

ISBN-10: 0-7910-8694-1
ISBN-13: 978-0-7910-8694-0

Library of Congress Cataloging-in-Publication Data
Parr, Ann.
  The Allisons / Ann Parr.
      p. cm. – (Race car legends. Collector's edition)
  Includes bibliographical references and index.
  ISBN-13: 978-0-7910-8694-0 (hardcover)
  ISBN-10: 0-7910-8694-1 (hardcover)
  1. Allison family—Juvenile literature. 2. Automobile racing drivers–United States–Biography—Juvenile literature. I. Title. II. Series.
  GV1032.A1P37 2007   796.720922–dc22
  [B]   2006100047

Chelsea House books are available at special discounts when purchased in bulk quantities for businesses, associations, institutions, or sales promotions. Please call our Special Sales Department in New York at (212) 967-8800 or (800) 322-8755.

You can find Chelsea House on the World Wide Web at http://www.chelseahouse.com

Series design by Erika K. Arroyo
Cover design by Hierophant Publishing Services/EON PreMedia/Joo Young An

Printed in the United States of America

Bang PH 10 9 8 7 6 5 4 3 2 1

This book is printed on acid-free paper.

All links and Web addresses were checked and verified to be correct at the time of publication. Because of the dynamic nature of the Web, some addresses and links may have changed since publication and may no longer be valid.

CONTENTS

1 The Allison Way   7

2 It Runs in the Family   15

3 Up Through the Ranks   23

4 Setbacks   31

5 Davey's Own Race   39

6 Unplanned Legacies   49

7 Getting on with Life   58

Statistics   63

Chronology   65

Glossary   67

Bibliography   69

Further Reading   70

Picture Credits   73

Index   74

About the Author   77

1

THE ALLISON WAY

Whenever Bobby Allison lost the Daytona 500 during his 18 years of racing, he missed by only a few seconds. On February 19, 1978, holding the lead, Bobby roared ahead at full throttle, not taking any chances. He crossed the finish line ahead of racer Cale Yarborough.

Bobby's sons—Davey and Clifford, 16 and 13 years old, respectively—and his wife, Judy, jumped and yelled and slapped each other high fives. Davey wasn't far from driving his first major race. Clifford, also interested in racing, wanted to be a jockey and race horses. The boys dashed down to the track toward their father.

A big win like this was never easy. During the **qualifying time** the day before, a car had slid into Bobby. The crash turned Bobby's big Thunderbird, nicknamed the "Luxury Liner," into a twisted pile of metal. If he were able to drive the next day's race at all, he would be in the thirty-third position at the starting line. Bobby stared at the mess, his hope fading. But his crew worked all night and made the car like new. "If these guys can do that for me," Bobby

Bobby Allison and his wife Judy hold aloft the Daytona 500 trophy in Victory Lane after Bobby's Daytona 500 win in 1978.

thought when he saw the car, "I'm going to drive that car the best I can."

The first crash during the race occurred at about lap 68. Another car's tire blew, sending cars in all directions.

Bobby slid into his neighbor but was able to keep going. At lap 117, Bobby tried to pass a competitor and ended up sandwiched between the other car and the wall of the track. Both sides of the Luxury Liner were damaged. The bent fender chewed into Bobby's front tire, requiring a **pit stop** for a replacement. The steering wheel, twisted during the squeeze, caused problems during the rest of the race. But neither problem slowed Bobby down. With 18 laps to go, he and racer Buddy Baker fought for first and second place until Baker's engine blew, and he was left behind. Bobby sprinted to the finish line ahead of Yarborough.

Years before, when Davey and Clifford were about six and three years old, respectively, they were in Elko, Minnesota, watching as their dad gained on his opponents, inch by inch. Suddenly, smoke and dust shot into the air. Bobby had sailed into a concrete wall after skidding on a patch of oil. The crash cost him 11 broken bones. Doctors sewed more than 40 stitches to repair his right eye, cheek, and lip. After five days in the hospital, Bobby headed back to the racetrack. In February of that same year, Bobby had wrecked his car at the Carolina 500 race in Rockingham, North Carolina, and had ended up in the hospital. Again, he climbed out of bed and immediately returned to the racetrack.

Bobby Allison—this father, husband, and brother—never used setbacks as excuses. "Can't do" was unacceptable as an answer; the harder the challenge, the greater his effort.

BOBBY'S BEGINNINGS

Bobby was born December 3, 1937, in Miami, Florida, the fifth of 13 children, ready to charge ahead. He owned a driver's license at age 14. He bought his first car and raced in circles around an empty field on the way home from school. Faster and faster he went, until he could spin out. He loved the excitement. As a senior in high school, he began racing at the Hialeah Speedway, a local Florida track. He finished tenth against 54 other racers, an impressive showing for a beginner. He also broke a record at Hialeah—not for speed, but for rolling his car twice. Bobby was well into cars by now—speeding, spinning, and rolling—and his parents weren't happy about it. Fearing for their son's safety, they forbade him to race again. He obeyed but did not leave his love of racing far behind.

Fisherman Bobby Allison, age 10, proudly displays his catch.

Following high school graduation in 1955, Bobby took a job testing outboard motorboat engines for Mercury Outboard. The Wisconsin-based company also owned a famous team of **stock car** racers. Bobby's boss transferred him to Charlotte, North Carolina, to be a mechanic on the pit crew. Bobby learned all he could about making motors run faster. Most of all, he learned the business side of racing.

Bobby quit his job with Mercury Outboard, returned to Florida, and bought a new 1956 Chevrolet. He began driving the local Florida tracks. He wanted to qualify for the **NASCAR** circuit. If Bobby wasn't on the racetrack, he was in his garage, finding ways to make his car run better. One

Bobby Allison waves a checkered flag from the Chevy he raced in Florida during the late 1950s.

day his car's automatic transmission slipped from a hoist, crushing his fingers. While recuperating, Bobby decided that if he was going to get hurt, he might as well be doing something he liked. From then on, Bobby's career would be racing. Nothing would get in his way then or later.

Once, at the track in Huntsville, Alabama, four drivers ganged up to run Bobby's car off the track. For the entire race, they surrounded his car and knocked into him from all sides. Between heats, he asked the drivers to lay off and give him room to pass on the track. They denied trying to block him. Bobby decided to take action. He quickly knocked the first driver out of the race. Next, he bumped the second car. It spun onto the infield. Finally, he pulled alongside the third car and quickly whirled his steering wheel to the right. The car dived into the wall. NASCAR officials fined Bobby for his actions, but Bobby didn't have any more trouble with those drivers.

THE ALLISON WAY: RACING

Following his retirement after a disabling racing accident in 1988, Bobby began traveling the country, speaking to young people and appearing at events for charity groups. He urged

THE FIRST DAYTONA RACE

The first race on Daytona Beach, the site of the famous Daytona 500, was in 1902. Ransom E. Olds, the founder of the Oldsmobile car company, drove the sand-packed beach in a timed run. Shortly after, he told his friend, "You have no idea what a thrill it is out there! Do you know what it feels like to go 50 miles an hour?"

The race ended with the two vehicles side by side. Each driver said it was a tie.

others to stick up for themselves. "I haven't seen anybody make any kind of successful continuance [progress] in life by refusing to accept what's happened," Bobby said. "To go and hide, to me, would be refusing to accept it."

Bobby Allison gets dowsed in Victory Lane after winning the Firecracker 400 race at the Daytona International Speedway in July 1987. Less than a year later, he was fighting for his life after being critically injured in a racing accident.

Bobby has had many reasons to hide. It took years to recover from brain damage and memory loss caused by the wreck that made him leave racing. That's not the worst of it, though. His sons, Davey and Clifford, were killed in race-related accidents in 1992 and 1993. For several months afterward, Bobby rarely was seen outside his home in Hueytown, Alabama. When asked how he was doing, he would just say that the sun would come up tomorrow, and he was taking it one day at a time.

"It's time to put the negatives behind us and get back where we belong," he told a group in 1995. "It's time to move on."

For Bobby Allison, moving on meant only one thing. Racing. He invested in Bobby Allison Motorsports, fielding his own race cars. He consulted for racing teams, and he coached young drivers. "Racing is the opportunity to do well through personal effort, personal commitment," Bobby explained to one of his audiences. "Making the right choices. . . . We have to keep looking for the next good time."

That's the Allison Way.

2

🏁

IT RUNS
IN THE FAMILY

Before the start of the 1988 Daytona 500, fans asked Bobby Allison what he planned to do if he found himself in the lead. "Hold it down and keep going," Bobby replied, "and dare the other guy to make a try at me." He didn't realize that, at the very last lap, he would be up against his own son, Davey.

THE ALLISONS START RACING

The Allison name had first became known in racing circles more than 25 years earlier. Bobby and his brother Donnie raced at smaller short tracks—shorter than one mile—in Florida and Alabama. They soon moved on to larger, faster **superspeedways**, and finally, to tracks like the Daytona International Speedway.

E.J. and Kittie, Bobby and Donnie's parents, closely followed their sons' racing. They traveled with the "Alabama Gang"—the nickname for a group of NASCAR drivers who operated out of Hueytown, Alabama. At the 1988 Daytona 500, spectators would have a chance to see this racing family at its best. The Daytona 500 is the first race

15

of the **Winston Cup** season. In 1988, Bobby went into the race as an old pro. At 50 years old, he already had won the Daytona twice. In contrast, 26-year-old Davey was competing for only the second time.

Davey had created a stir in the racing world. He was named 1987 NASCAR **Rookie of the Year**. He also became the first rookie ever to start the Daytona 500 from the first row, a new record at 1987's Daytona. In 1988, he once again qualified for a place in the front row, a few rows ahead of his father.

1987 NASCAR Rookie of the Year Davey Allison waits while his car is checked after a practice run.

When the flagman waved the green **flag**, Bobby and Davey darted away from the starting line and were soon racing side by side, lap after lap. Bobby gained the lead and pushed through a wall of air. This left a nice, clear pocket of air for **drafting**. As cars pulled into that pocket, they were sucked along. But Bobby benefited, too. To gain position, others had to go around him. The drivers following Bobby had to figure out how to break out of the draft to pass other cars, a move known as "**slingshotting**."

Bobby clearly had a strong, well-built car. Most drivers who were drafting were unable to work up enough speed to slingshot past him. Throughout the race, while other cars were falling apart and falling behind, Bobby's Buick Regal remained comfortably in the lead.

MOONSHINE AND NASCAR

When alcoholic beverages were outlawed during Prohibition, some people made their own, called moonshine. Those who made moonshine sometimes had to run from the law. Many people built regular-looking but souped-up cars that could outrun the police. When there was no government agent around to chase them, the moonshine makers raced each other up and down the roads and on the short dirt tracks in the area. By the late 1930s, these fast cars had gone to the beaches of Daytona, Florida.

The story of moonshine is woven into the history of NASCAR, and included in popular entertainment about car racing. The movie *Smokey and the Bandit* and the television series *The Dukes of Hazzard* show Southern guys in fast cars running illegal liquor. The movie *Days of Thunder* shows Tom Cruise's character celebrating his first victory by drinking moonshine from a glass jar.

With about 10 laps to go, Bobby looked in his rear view mirror and saw one car strong enough to make the pass. It was his son Davey's car. Davey slingshotted out of the draft and closed up the distance Bobby had tried to put between them. As the two cars raced toward the finish line, they were side by side, close enough to see each other behind the wheel. Davey had his car running at full speed, but his Thunderbird could not match the momentum his father's Buick had built. The checkered flag sliced through the air, signaling the end of the race. Bobby crossed the finish line first. Davey roared in only a second later.

When asked whether he considered just letting his father win, Davey said, "Since I was a kid I've dreamed about a down-to-the-wire battle with Dad. But in my dreams I won." When asked years later which race was his favorite, Davey said it was not one of his many victories that meant the most to him. It was the race in which he came in second, when he had the honor of losing to his father—the great Bobby Allison.

BOBBY AND DONNIE'S EARLY RACES

Bobby and his brother Donnie, sons of a service-station equipment supplier, grew up in Miami, Florida. From the time they were young, they loved to go to the racetrack to experience the thrills and excitement of the sport. In 1959, the brothers decided to leave Miami. They competed primarily in divisions known as the modifieds. These races were known as the testing grounds for young drivers hoping to make it into NASCAR's major league, the **Grand Nationals**. The cars in the modified races, unlike the slick, professionally built newer models in the Grand Nationals, were older models that the drivers souped up

Brothers Bobby *(left)* and Donnie Allison not only raced cars, they
learned how engines worked and made their own repairs.

themselves. Bobby and Donnie had to rebuild their cars
after each race. Sometimes they could barely afford to pay
for the parts they needed. Bobby once showed up at a race
in Richmond, Virginia, without enough money to pay for
tires. He borrowed a set from another driver.

Bobby and Donnie raced up to five nights a week,
hoping to win enough money to be able to race again the
following week. They often had to drive all night and all
day to make it to the next race on time—and then they

had to hop into a race car and do their best with only a couple of hours of sleep. The modified circuit was rough. The drivers were fiercely competitive both on and off the track. The local drivers ganged up on drivers from out of town and tried to knock them out of the race.

Bobby Allison sits on the hood of his '66 Chevy after winning a 25-mile race at the Daytona Speedway in 1968.

Donnie Allison poses by his number 1 stock car after ranking number one in the qualifying runs for pole position in the 1977 Daytona 500.

Eventually, Bobby and Donnie settled down in Hueytown, Alabama, mostly because it was close to the modified racing circuit of the southeastern United States. That circuit stretched from northern Louisiana through the Carolinas to Virginia and included many tracks that provided plenty of chances for the brothers to race. Bobby and Donnie competed almost every night of the week.

During those years, Bobby and Donnie saw just about every kind of situation that could develop in a race. They also saw the different ways drivers handled these incidents. Most importantly, they learned which strategies worked and which didn't. When Bobby was in a race and a problem came up, he learned to make split-second decisions about what to do. Also, because they made all their own repairs, the brothers developed a keen understanding of how cars operate. This understanding helped Bobby fix his car to improve its performance. When the car wasn't running properly, Bobby knew how to use his driving skills to make up for the problem.

By 1965, Bobby and Donnie had mastered the modified circuit. Bobby had won the NASCAR subcategory of the modified special championship twice and also had won the modified championship twice. When an elderly car owner named Betty Lilly offered him an opportunity to drive her Ford, he decided he was ready to move up to the Grand Nationals.

3

![checkered flag]

UP THROUGH
THE RANKS

In 1966, Bobby competed at the quarter-mile track in Bowman Gray Stadium in Winston-Salem, North Carolina. Still a rookie in the Grand Nationals, he shocked the racing world by bumping the car of an experienced professional. Throughout the race, they continued knocking against one another. They forced each other to spin out of control and slam into the wall. Eventually, they knocked each other out of the race. Bobby had learned how to ignore the unwritten guidelines in racing—whom you can hit and how hard, and who you must allow to pass you. He became known for his aggressive, hard-charging driving style. His reputation on the racetrack was set.

Off the track, Bobby was friendly, warm, and charming. He became one of the most popular racers on the circuit among both fans and fellow drivers. After each race, he met with his admirers. He considered them friends, and he listened to their praise and even their criticism. By 1982, he had been voted the most popular Grand National driver four times in NASCAR polls. On the track, however, Bobby was quite a different person. His personal motto was "whatever it takes." He raced to win.

BOBBY BATTLES RICHARD PETTY

Bobby proved his reputation during one of the most famous feuds in racing history. Richard Petty won the Winston Cup Series championship seven times. He also won the Daytona 500 seven times, far more than any other driver. "Petty was established, the top guy, and I was just coming on," Bobby said, describing the early rivalry in a biography of Petty titled *King Richard*. "He seemed to take the attitude he shouldn't be challenged. But I go into every race with the intention of doing whatever it takes to win and so does he."

"King" Richard Petty gives the victory sign after winning a NASCAR race in Trenton, New Jersey, in 1970. The competition between Bobby Allison and Richard Petty became a years-long rivalry, spurring both drivers to greatness.

In 1967, Bobby was only a rookie on the Grand National circuit. By then, Petty had earned the nickname "King." Late in the season, a minor fender bender happened between the two drivers. It was unclear which driver had caused the accident. The following summer, another incident led

Bobby Allison shows off his trophy after ending Richard Petty's seven-race winning streak at the 1974 Richmond 500 at the Fairgrounds Raceway in Richmond, Virginia.

to a fistfight between their two crews. Petty and Bobby each blamed the other for starting the feud. Each claimed he had only reacted to a move initiated by the other. From then on, Bobby didn't hesitate to knock Petty around. "We got to looking for each other, if you know what I mean. It just went on and on," Bobby said. For five years, at both short track and Grand National superspeedway races, they would bump against one another on the track. At times, their disputes led to major pileups. Eventually, the two met in person and worked out their differences.

BOBBY BATTLES DONNIE

Bobby and Donnie's competition was another great rivalry for fans. Donnie had moved up to the Grand National circuit in 1966 and was making a name for himself. In 1967, he finished in the top 10 in seven different races and was nominated Rookie of the Year. In 1968, he did even better, finishing in the top 5 in five different races. While the brothers often had faced one another on short tracks, they now raced each other in major events. On several occasions, the race came down to a "last lap" Allison-versus-Allison showdown.

One of these was the National 500 at the Charlotte Speedway in October 1969. During the first lap, Donnie quickly took the lead. He held it for much of the race. Bobby, in a Daytona Charger, stayed close behind him. The only other driver to stay close was Buddy Baker, in a Dodge Daytona. With only five laps left in the race, Baker ran out of gas and dropped out. That left Donnie and Bobby battling it out for the win in the final laps.

Bobby's Charger managed to creep up on Donnie's Ford Talladega. Bobby pulled up alongside Donnie and tried to pass him. Donnie crossed the finish line seconds ahead of his brother. "People ask me who's the best driver I ever raced against, and it's got to be Donnie," Bobby said.

In 1970 Donnie entered racing history books by finishing fourth in the Indianapolis 500 at Indianapolis Motor Speedway, and then winning the World 600 at Charlotte Motor Speedway—remarkably, in the same weekend. He is noted as the most successful cross-over driver (going from stock cars to Indy cars) in history. He was awarded the 1967 Rookie of the Year, the 1970 Indianapolis Rookie of the

Donnie Allison earned a reputation as one of the most successful drivers to cross over from racing stock cars to racing IndyCars. Donnie is shown in his race car at the Indianapolis Motor Speedway in 1971.

Year, and the 1970 Sportsman Most Popular Driver honor. He has 10 Winston Cup wins in 239 starts, has finished 78 times in the top 5, and has finished 115 times in the top 10.

The 1971 Winston 500 featured one of the great NASCAR finishes of all time, a classic Allison-versus-Allison moment.

BOBBY ALLISON, DESIGNER AND INVENTOR

When Bobby Allison began racing, drivers worked on their own cars, even building them from the ground up. Throughout the years, Bobby developed new and better ways to build high performance racers. He became a designer and an inventor as well as a race car driver. During 1959, he invented a split-spring suspension system for modifieds. It allowed for lighter cars and gave a driver better control over the car. During 1966, he designed a modern, front-steering chassis for Winston Cup and Busch cars. Most drivers use this chassis today. During the 1980s, he designed an aircraft propeller-loaded-dyno for Winston Cup and Busch engines. He also designed an oil heated wing de-ice, anti-ice system for light twin-engine airplanes. He converted his own Superstar airplane engine from a piston-powered engine to a turbine-powered engine.

Bobby Allison *(right)* tinkers in the workshop while brothers Eddie *(left)* and Donnie watch.

Donnie Allison enjoys the moment after beating his brother Bobby to win the 1971 Winston 500 at the Alabama International Speedway, Talladega, Alabama. In 1989, the track was renamed Talladega Superspeedway.

Bobby and Donnie were both driving Mercury models, and they kept battling for the lead with Buddy Baker and Dave Marcis, who were both driving Dodges. By the last 70 miles of the 500-mile race, each of the four drivers had held the lead at some point.

With only eight laps to the end, Marcis's engine caught fire. That left Donnie in the lead, with Buddy Baker and brother Bobby right behind. The race came down to the final lap, with the three almost side by side. Coming out of the final turn of the final lap, Donnie pulled slightly ahead of the other two. He sailed into the home stretch and won by one car length.

Bobby went on to have his own spectacular season, one of the best of his career. He earned seven NASCAR super-speedway victories. During that year he nearly doubled all his previous winnings. But that 1971 Allison-versus-Allison finish proved that Donnie was an excellent racer in his own right. "Donnie just didn't race as much as I did," Bobby said.

4

SETBACKS

In the final race of 1983, Bobby only needed a decent finish to take the Winston Cup. He finished ninth, good enough to make him the season's champ. It was NASCAR's top award. Bobby considered it the highlight of his career.

The win was testimony to Bobby's perseverance. It had taken more than 20 years of racing to reach that moment. In 1981 and 1982, he came in second, losing by only a handful of points. But Bobby wasn't discouraged by those close losses. Each year, he came back more determined to do his best.

BOBBY'S SETBACKS

The worst slump of Bobby's career, a dry period in the late 1970s, is still known as one of the worst in racing history. The trouble started in 1976 with two serious crashes only four months apart. At the Carolina 500 in February and at a short track in Elko, Minnesota, a few months later, Bobby suffered injuries that landed him in the hospital. He returned to the track as soon as he could manage.

The following season, 1977, was an all-time low for Bobby. He lacked energy and experienced intense stomach pains. But he remained in the competition. "Time to put

1983 Winston Cup champion Bobby Allison embraces his parents, E.J. and Kitty, at the Daytona International Speedway, Daytona Beach, Florida.

on the best act of your life," he said to himself. "When you get to **Victory Lane**, don't show these people how terrible you feel."

After the two accidents, Bobby raced in 67 races without a single win. Two straight seasons with no wins only made Bobby more determined. Yet mysterious attacks of a stomach illness continued to plague him. "Needless to say, both emotionally and physically, I was at a real low spot then," Bobby said about the approaching 1978 season. "I really didn't know what I was going to do, so I considered running the short tracks full time."

At the end of a long day in his shop, Bobby flopped into a recliner in his den. The stomach problems were taking over. The telephone rang. He struggled out of the

Bobby Allison's wrecked stock car is shown after a crash that occurred at the North Carolina Motor Speedway. Allison and seven other drivers tangled on the backstretch of the track during the 1976 Carolina 500.

chair to answer it. Car owner Bud Moore was on the line. "Look," he said, "I know you've been doing lousy, and I've been doing lousy, and I think we ought to see if we can get together." Moore knew of Bobby's abilities and past victories. Despite Bobby's slump, Moore believed in him as a driver. He hired Bobby to drive his car—a big Thunderbird that he nicknamed the Luxury Liner.

In the first race for Moore, Bobby crashed. Then, in the qualifying race for the Daytona 500, he crashed again. He was nauseated and feeling terrible. He went to the

Daytona track on Saturday to tell Moore he was going home to Hueytown, and that he would not be driving for him after all. He entered the garage to look for Moore. The Luxury Liner that he had wrecked the day before gleamed with white and blue paint, still too wet to touch. The car had been brought back to life, and Bobby knew he had to drive it. Even with a starting position of 33, Bobby and the Luxury Liner won that 1978 Daytona 500. What better race could he win to put an end to a 67-race losing streak?

RACERS UNDERSTAND EACH OTHER

Neil Bonnett was a dear friend of the Allisons and an Alabama Gang member who died in a practice lap crash at Daytona in 1994.

Neil Bonnett and Bobby Allison were sitting at Davey Allison's funeral in 1993, when they looked at each other. Neil was planning to get back in a race car and Bobby was itching to drive again after recovering from an accident. They just smiled, knowing that no one else would understand the urge to race. They agreed that they could never explain it. They determined that nothing could make a person get back into car racing if he didn't want to—and that nothing could keep a person out of a car if he really wanted to drive.

Members of NASCAR's "Alabama Gang" included (*from left*) Neil Bonnett, Donnie Allison, and Bobby Allison. All hailed from Hueytown, Alabama.

Still recovering from injuries and trying to regain his strength, Bobby won four more Winston Cup races in 1978 and finished second in the Winston Cup standings. And he finally learned what was wrong with his stomach—a hernia condition that could be controlled by medication.

A STRONG STARTING SEASON

In December 1981, Bobby signed with a new team— DiGard/Gatorade. The crew admired Bobby as a driver and gave him a great deal of encouragement. Right from the start of the 1982 season, Bobby came on strong. As always, the first race of the season was the Daytona 500. The big day gave Bobby and his new team a real workout.

Bobby Allison smiles as he prepares for a race in his DiGard/Gatorade race car.

After the fourth lap, Bobby made his move and pulled in front. But then, 10 miles into the race, Cale Yarborough hit Bobby from behind, sending the bumper of Bobby's car flying onto the track. Five other cars knocked into the bumper and skidded off the track and out of the race. Driving without a bumper seriously affected how well Bobby could control the car. But Bobby used his driving know-how and maintained his speed. He held the lead for 147 of the 200 laps.

About halfway through the race, another car blew its engine, sending shrapnel-like pieces of scrap metal and car parts flying into the air and into Bobby's car. The burning engine of that car created a thick cloud of smoke. As Bobby came around a turn, he drove directly into the smoke, leaving him unable to see where he was going or what awaited him on the track ahead. "I couldn't see nothing but smoke," Bobby later told *Sports Illustrated.* "I mean *nothing.* I couldn't see the racetrack, the other cars, the wall, *nothing.* So I just squeezed up against the wall and held my breath."

Other cars spun all over the track, blindly smashing into one another. Late in the race, Darrell Waltrip came up behind Bobby and tried to pass him to take the lead. Bobby had lost the Winston Cup crown to Waltrip the year before, which made him especially determined to beat Waltrip in the current race.

After Waltrip passed by, several other drivers also followed in the draft behind him. Bobby joined the line, now in fifth place. Suddenly, Waltrip's engine blew, too. Bobby quickly took advantage of the situation. Under the cover of the cloud of smoke caused by Waltrip's engine, he pulled out of the draft and slingshotted ahead of the others. With about 50 miles left in the race, Bobby held the lead by about a mile. Finally, with only half a mile to go, Bobby's engine began to sputter. He was running out of gas. For a second, he panicked, remembering the previous year's Daytona, when, only seconds from winning the race, he had run out of gas. Bobby pushed the accelerator and prayed he would make it. He did run out of fuel, but not until he had crossed the finish line. It was his second Daytona win, making him only the third driver, after Yarborough and Petty, to win the Daytona more than once.

Bobby Allison takes the checkered flag for his second Daytona 500 win. He piloted his Buick to victory over a starting field of 42 cars.

BOBBY TAKES ON THE WORLD

Bobby said his most satisfying race of 1982 was not the Daytona 500. It was a race he didn't even win. The World 600 is the longest race on the NASCAR circuit and is considered by many to be the most difficult. The conditions are particularly grueling, as it takes place in Charlotte, North Carolina, in May, when the temperature can reach 90° F (32° C) or higher. The heat generated by a car engine and its exhaust pipes can raise the temperature inside the car to well above 100° F. Halfway through this race, the exhaust pipes on Bobby's Buick broke off, causing the floorboards of his car to heat to nearly 1,000° F (538° C). Poisonous exhaust fumes blew into the car, but he somehow managed to complete the race.

Bobby decided that, having recovered from his stomach problems and regaining his strength, he was now once again one of the best in his sport. Bobby proudly told *Sports Illustrated* that he now thought he was the toughest.

5

DAVEY'S OWN RACE

For Bobby's sons, Davey and Clifford, the racetrack was a second home. From the time they were little, they attended races with their parents and two sisters, Bonnie and Carrie. They all cheered for Bobby and their uncle Donnie.

Davey was born the day before the February 26, 1961, Daytona 500. Bobby was driving a qualifying event on February 24 when he received word that his wife, Judy, was in labor. He jumped into his pickup truck and sped to the hospital in Davie, Florida, where Judy gave birth to Davey on February 25. Bobby rushed back to the racetrack and finished thirty-first in the Daytona 500 on February 26. Bobby's second son, Clifford, was born October 20, 1964.

Davey was single-minded, headed for a racing career from the time he learned to ride a tricycle. Clifford was a fun-loving and carefree little boy. The boys built a bike track in a wooded area across from the family home. They competed against each other and against friends in the neighborhood. Colored flags signaled the starts and finishes of the races, just as if they were professional. When each Allison

Judy and Bobby Allison pose trackside with their four children, *(from left)* Clifford, Bonnie, Carrie and Davey.

boy chose which professional racer he would pretend to be, Davey chose Bobby every time. And he won every time. His purple bicycle became a legend in the neighborhood.

"Davey and Clifford used to come into the shop on tricycles racing each other," a family friend said. "We'd be in here working on race cars, and we'd have to run them out. Davey was always the competitor. Clifford was the world's best at taking things apart and the world's worst at putting them together. I remember he took his daddy's riding lawnmower apart, and it never got put back together."

Davey looked forward to the day when he could follow his father's example and make his racing dreams come true. He attended summer school and graduated from Hueytown High School in January 1979, four months ahead of his class. He wanted to race as soon as he could.

Davey Allison *(left)* and his grandfather, E.J. "Pop" Allison, are shown working as part of the pit crew and waiting to service Bobby's car.

Clifford did not plan to pursue car racing as his father and brother had. At first, he wanted to be a jockey on racehorses. But by the time he had healed from a serious motorcycle accident that hurt his left leg, he was too tall to qualify as a jockey. He joined Davey and a few friends to form their own racing team. Bobby nicknamed them "The Peach Fuzz Gang" because none of them had started shaving yet. The Peach Fuzz Gang traveled to tracks all over the Southeast.

TAKING A BREAK

About halfway through a race, drivers begin to feel tired. They start to lose concentration. Their legs need to be stretched. They may be getting hungry or thirsty. Their arms are sore from controlling the car. If the weather is hot, they may need a breath of cooler air. On very hot days, drivers can suffer from heat stroke and even faint. You might think drivers get a break during pit stops, but they don't. A pit stop is short (20 or fewer seconds), and drivers are busy listening to instructions or telling their crew chiefs about the car. So what can drivers do when they need to rest?

Drivers radio their crew chiefs through a microphone inside their helmets. They tell them what they need. Drivers hear their crew chiefs through an earpiece. Sometimes drivers tell their crew chiefs they want a relief driver. Then another driver takes over, either for a few laps or for the rest of the race, even though it takes precious time to make the switch: one driver out; one driver in; fasten seat belts; and listen to last-minute instructions. When this takes place, only the first driver receives the NASCAR points.

DAVEY MAKES A LASTING IMPRESSION

Davey used every race to learn more. At almost every event, Davey would skid along the fence or veer off into the grandstand. His car suffered all kinds of wear and tear. But he'd go home, talk to his dad, and work night and day to put the car back together. A week later, he'd be ready for another race, and ready to learn the next lesson.

From Davey's first race—April 22, 1979, in Birmingham, Alabama—he made a lasting impression. Driving a 1972 Chevy Nova that he'd borrowed from his uncle Donnie,

Bobby Allison adjusts Davey's chin strap in this undated family photograph.

he came in fifth—an astonishing finish for a young driver who lacked experience. Five races later, he amazed even more spectators by coming in first.

In the early 1980s, Davey had a string of wins while racing in a series run by the Automobile Racing Club of American (ARCA). Through trial and error, he sharpened his talents and gained experience. He began to win more and more races until, in 1985, he was named ARCA's all-time leader in superspeedway wins. He became even more serious about following his father's footsteps. Beginning in 1985, Davey made his debut in Winston Cup racing at the track in Talladega, Alabama, close to his home in Hueytown. He finished tenth, a truly impressive beginning. In 1986, car owner Junior Johnston asked Davey to take over for his driver in a Winston Cup race. Davey loved the challenge. Using what he had learned, he pulled into the lead. Some drivers passed him, but he regained the lead and finished seventh. His performance attracted more attention.

Davey stormed onto the NASCAR scene at the 1987 Daytona 500. Running at exceptionally high speeds, he qualified to participate in the race. He also earned a first-row spot—quite a feat for a rookie. After this sudden success at the start of the season, Davey ran the super-speedway in Darlington, South Carolina. It was known as one of the most dangerous tracks in the circuit. Davey's car and another car smashed into one another. Davey skidded off the course, spinning rapidly as he plowed through some wooden poles. An explosion followed, and his car burst into flames. Davey escaped without serious injury. He took a deep breath and looked around for the car he had hit, and did a double take. He had crashed into his father, the great Bobby Allison. He was now racing with the big boys.

Family traditions continue as Kyle Petty *(right)*, son of Richard Petty, meets with Davey Allison to wish him luck before the 1983 Quaker State 150 race at Pocono International Raceway in Long Pond, Pennsylvania. Petty drove in another race at the track the following day.

A month later, Davey once again entered a race with his father. They met at what they thought of as their "home track" at Talladega. This time, though, it was Bobby who became involved in a near-death crash. About 21 laps into the race, Bobby's car flew into the air. It flipped over before crashing into the dirt. Davey checked his rearview mirror. He panicked at the sight and feared the worst. He couldn't imagine his father had survived that crash. He also feared that other cars would plow into his father while Davey circled the track. As he came around the turn, Bobby waved at him to signal that he was okay. Davey whooped and hollered in celebration—and kept going.

Feeling relieved, Davey sailed on to the finish line, earning himself a spot in Victory Lane. That year he became the first rookie since 1981 to win a Winston Cup race. A few weeks later, another win at the track in Dover, Delaware, helped him earn the title Rookie of the Year. Clearly, there was a new Allison making headlines.

Davey's second year of Winston Cup racing, 1988, began with his famous second-place finish against his father at the Daytona 500. Before the race, Davey said he planned to use some of his father's tricks to win. He soon found out that his father hadn't taught him all his tricks.

In those first few years on the Winston Cup circuit, Davey earned several wins. His many victories, as well as his charm, energy, and youthful enthusiasm won over many fans. In the racing world, though, Davey gained a reputation for being unpredictable. Like his father, Davey was a tough driver, willing to take risks. Sometimes, though, Davey's aggression prevented him from thinking clearly. He would wind up right in the middle of a major smashup that could have been avoided.

In the middle of the 1991 season, Larry McReynolds became Davey's crew chief and the leader of his team. McReynolds knew that Davey's greatest strength was his aggressiveness, but that it was also his biggest weakness. McReynolds showed Davey that by holding back at times, he could make his chances of winning much greater. The new team, led by McReynolds, worked very well together. With this new team, Davey won 11 of his 19 career victories. Unlike his father, Davey found a team he liked early on in his career.

Just how much Davey had matured as a driver became clear to everyone at the start of the 1992 season, at the Daytona 500. A crash at a turn into the backstretch involved nearly half the drivers. The crash occurred when three drivers entered the turn at a point where the track narrows down to two lanes. One driver tried to slow down and drop back, but it was too late. As the track narrowed,

Davey Allison edges out Morgan Shepherd and crosses the finish line to win the 1992 Daytona 500.

that driver's car was sandwiched between the two other cars. All three spun out of control. As other cars sped out of the turn, the drivers headed directly into a whirlpool of cars. The crash, a 14-car pileup, became one of the largest in Daytona history.

Davey, however, was not in one of the crashing cars. He had been behind the three that were the first to crash and could have stayed there. However, he remembered that cars cannot make the fast turns at Daytona three abreast. He held back. Bobby was proud of Davey's good judgment. Davey knew that a year earlier, he probably would have been right at the center of the pileup. "But I've grown up a lot," he told reporters. Throughout the race, Davey had demonstrated smart yet tough driving. He managed to hold the lead for a remarkable 127 laps of the 200-lap race and won, earning his place in Victory Lane as his father had done three times before.

6

UNPLANNED LEGACIES

The Allison Way was daring and risky. Though that way often led to victories, it also included disappointments, tragedies, and death. In 1981, Donnie was involved in a major crash in a race in Charlotte, North Carolina. Although he had survived many minor crashes during his career, this was more serious. In addition to bumps and bruises, he suffered damaging injuries to his head. He tried to continue racing but found it too difficult. A few weeks later, he retired from active race car driving.

After Bobby's February 1988 Daytona victory over his son Davey, the rest of the season not only changed his life, but also abruptly ended his successful career. During the first lap of his 717th appearance in a Winston Cup race, on June 19, he realized that something was wrong. "I think I've got a right rear tire going down," Bobby told his crew over the radio. "Get one ready. I'm coming in."

But he didn't make it in. As he drove into the second turn, his car broke loose and smacked the outside wall. Bobby swung his head to the left and spotted a racer's worst nightmare. Several cars, traveling at speeds

Donnie Allison waves to fans as he is introduced before the start of a NASCAR Busch race in March 2006, at the Atlanta Motor Speedway in Hampton, Georgia.

of 170 miles per hour, were charging right toward him. They knocked into his Buick, smashing it into the fence. One car slammed into Bobby's driver's-side door. A radio announcer yelled that it was the hardest hit in a car race that he'd ever seen in his life. Davey Allison, in the same race, saw the commotion. He radioed his crew, "What's going on? Is Dad involved?"

"Davey, it's your dad, and I've got to tell you it doesn't look good," they answered. It wasn't good.

A paramedic climbed into Bobby's car and cut a hole in the front of his neck, into his windpipe, to help him breathe. It was an emergency decision that gave Bobby a thread of life from which to hang. Critically injured, with broken bones and bruises all over his body, he hovered close to death. Deep in a multi-month coma, he fought off death, just as he fought off competitors on the racetrack. After gaining consciousness, he had to relearn everything—walking, talking, brushing his teeth, getting dressed—everything. After months of recovery, he limped onto the track at Daytona in February 1989. Both Clifford and Davey were competing. "I . . . am . . . very . . . glad," Bobby said, with terrible difficulty, "that . . . both . . . Davey . . . and Clifford . . . are . . . out there . . . racing, . . . because . . . there is . . . a lot . . . more good . . . out there . . . than . . . bad."

"I meant that," Bobby said later, when his speech had improved. "I still believe that."

Bobby's recovery astounded his family, his doctors, even himself. He walked with a slight limp, his balance was shaky, and his memory had blank spots. Perhaps thankfully, he didn't remember the race that ended his career. But, sadly, neither did he remember the 1988 Daytona 500 that he won when his son, Davey, came in second. He did not race again. When asked whether his career had been worth all this, Bobby said, "I don't know why it had to happen. I don't know why it had to happen the way it did. But my racing career has been worth it."

TWO DEADLY CRASHES

In July 1990, Davey raced in Pocono, Pennsylvania, at the very same track where his father had crashed. As Davey made his way through a pack of cars, he collided with another car. Skidding to the center of the track, Davey's car flipped over and over 11 times before it stopped. Parts flew all over the track until only a skeletonlike shell remained. Davey was tossed and turned inside. Miraculously, he survived. He spent the next several days in the hospital, recovering from a concussion, a broken arm, a broken collarbone, and broken ribs. "An accident like at Pocono brings you back down to earth and makes you realize we're all human and we're all very vulnerable," he stated.

Only six days after this accident, Davey got right back in his race car. He was terrified. His crew taped his hands to the steering wheel so that he could control the vehicle. He managed to complete five laps before turning the car over to another driver. To his crew, fellow racers, and fans, this was a sign of Davey's courage as well as a tribute to his family.

At age 27, Clifford was forging his own racing career in the Busch Grand National series. He showed great promise, with the same instinct for aggressive driving as his father and brother. "He had just turned a really fast lap in that practice session," Bobby said. "He came into the garage, and his crew made some minor adjustments. As he backed out of the garage, he looked at me and grinned, 'We're gonna get 'em, Dad.' His last words to me were, 'We're gonna get 'em, Dad,'" Bobby said, as his voice dwindled to a whisper.

Back on the track, Clifford zoomed down the backstretch of the two-mile track in Brooklyn, Michigan. His car broke loose and hit the wall head on. Efforts to revive him failed. He was pronounced dead in a nearby hospital.

Bobby had nurtured Clifford's climb through Busch Grand National racing. "Clifford was stimulating me so much," Bobby said about his own quickening recovery. Kittie Allison, Bobby's mother, said that working

Clifford Allison helps push his car to a staging area for a practice run at the Watkins Glen International racetrack near Watkins Glen, New York. Several weeks later, in August 1992, he lost his life during a crash at a Busch Grand National practice run in Brooklyn, Michigan.

with Clifford was Bobby's "therapy" during recovery. But after Clifford's death, she said, Bobby's recovery slowed.

ALL THE HEARTACHE

Clifford's death shocked Davey too. He took comfort the best way he knew how: He went ahead with his plan to race the next weekend. Many people criticized him, but Davey believed it was the best way to deal with his own grief. Davey managed to finish fifth in that race in Michigan, clearly the most difficult race of his career.

THE ALLISONS' TRUST IN GOD

The Allison family's faith gave them strength to make their way through many heartbreaking tragedies. Bobby and Donnie Allison's mother, Kittie, led the way as the family prayed after Bobby's injury and after the deaths of Clifford and Davey. "She always kept me aware that God was in control of everything," Bobby remembered.

One day during Bobby's slow and painful recovery from the Pocono accident, his priest asked him whether he remembered what he used to do before every takeoff in his airplane. Bobby slowly raised his hand and made the sign of the cross—two lines, one straight up and one across. Then his mother knew he would recover. She also knew that was the miracle she had expected. "That lady right over there," Donnie said, pointing to Kittie, "raised us to believe from the time we were little bitty kids that you put it in the good Lord's hands and you don't question His decisions."

After Clifford's death, Bobby turned his attention to Davey. They traveled together. They talked about old things and new things: Davey's outlook, his ambitions. They returned from a July 1993 New Hampshire race in their airplane. The next morning, Bobby went to his office to make some business phone calls. In the middle of one call, another phone line rang. His brother-in-law answered it. "Hang up the phone," he ordered Bobby. "And get that other line." He had never been so commanding with Bobby before.

The caller informed Bobby that Davey's helicopter had crashed at Talladega, where Davey had traveled to test a friend's car. "I went to the house and told Judy we had to go," Bobby said, at the time hoping the message was a mistake. "We got to the hospital in Birmingham before the rescue helicopter got there with Davey. They worked on Davey for about three hours. Then they said we'd have to wait and see." Just after dawn on July 13, 1993, Davey died.

The next morning, down at his racing shop, Bobby buried his face in the chest of a journalist he had known for a long time and wept hard. "It hurts!" he sobbed. Then he screamed, "Oh, it hurts. All the joy...all the success... now all the heartache."

Davey was only 32. His peers and fans agree that he would have gone on to greater glory on the track. He already had 19 Winston Cup wins, including the 1992 Daytona 500. His total winnings, $6.7 million, put him tenth on the all-time career list. The Sunday before his fatal accident, he had finished third in that race in London, New Hampshire, placing him fifth in the 1993 Winston Cup standing.

Davey Allison celebrates winning the 1992 Daytona 500. He was a contender for the Winston Cup in 1993 when he lost his life in a helicopter crash.

THE ALLISON WAY

A few days after Davey's funeral, Bobby's mother, Kittie, visited with a journalist. "There is some reason," she said, her eyes welling with tears, "some reason all of this has happened. We don't know what it is. But there's some reason. Someday we hope to find out." She paused, took a second to dry her tears, and said, "Don't you realize what a miracle we have? Just seeing Bobby. Don't you realize what a miracle it is?" Bobby's mother, Kittie, then in her nineties, was once again showing the family how to move on with hope and faith, no matter what.

Bobby and Donnie, after their accidents, squarely faced their limitations. They found new slots in the racing world. Donnie served as crew chief for other drivers and became co-announcer for the television networks ABC and CBS. Bobby fielded his own racing team.

Clifford gave racing his best in the last two years of his life. And Davey's future stood bright and promising. The Allison Way served the family in good times and in bad. The Allisons held their heads high, knowing they had shown racing their best. They did whatever it took with whatever they had.

7

GETTING ON
WITH LIFE

Bobby Allison began to build an impressive legacy from the time he and Donnie first drove the backroads of Florida at night from one race to another. They slept in the car and earned hardly any money, but they were doing what they loved. Bobby's love of racing helped shape NASCAR into the popular sport that it is today. Even those who didn't like his methods of winning admired Bobby's "never-give-up" attitude and actions. He was one of a kind.

Bobby was handed the toughest of life experiences. According to doctors and witnesses, it was amazing that he lived through the June 1988 crash. He used the same doggedness to overcome his injuries—paralysis and brain damage—but he never raced again. Losing two sons to the profession he loved on top of the life-robbing setback of his accident was almost too much. Not many would have blamed him if he had retreated to a rocking chair and nursed his hurts.

But Bobby forced himself to recover. His wife, Judy, wouldn't have had it otherwise, either. Bobby had reason to get out of bed and learn to walk and talk again.

NASCAR great Bobby Allison signs autographs for admiring fans. Allison helped shape NASCAR into the popular organization it is today.

Bobby and Judy faced huge doctor and hospital bills that their insurance companies refused to pay. Recovering opened up the possibility of Bobby's being paid to celebrate his legacy with his admiring public. He scheduled appearances, gave speeches, fielded his own race cars, and coached young drivers. All of this kept him in his beloved racing world and paid the medical debts.

Bobby recovered, with Judy leading the way. But finally—with the 1988 accident, the loss of two sons, and Bobby being who he was—Judy had had enough. Bobby and Judy divorced in 1996.

REMEMBERING NOT TO QUIT

When Richard Petty's grandson Adam was killed in a race car accident, Bobby and Judy agreed to put their differences aside long enough to help the Pettys. After all, the Allisons knew about losing precious family members to the sport of racing. More than a thousand friends and relatives showed up for Adam's funeral, but "the King," Richard Petty, knew the sacrifice Bobby and Judy had made, after a bitter divorce, to come together to help the Pettys in

Adam Petty *(right)* and his grandfather Richard Petty share a laugh after Adam's win in the 1998 Easy Care 100 ARCA race at the Charlotte Motor Speedway in Concord, North Carolina. Bobby and Judy Allison reunited to console the Pettys after Adam's tragic death at the age of 19.

Judy and Bobby Allison wave to fans at the Talladega Superspeedway during pre-race ceremonies honoring Davey Allison on the 10-year anniversary of his death.

their grief. Petty was touched. Afterward, Bobby said, "It's ironic that the Petty tragedy presented the opportunity for us, first of all, to speak to each other, and then to put our feelings aside to help someone else."

Bobby and Judy remarried in front of a judge on July 3, 2000. They scheduled a church ceremony to renew their wedding vows with family and friends on February 20, 2001. That would have been their fortieth wedding anniversary.

But instead of the renewal of vows, the Allisons attended the funeral of Dale Earnhardt, who was killed in a racing accident on February 18. Once again, tragedy intervened in their lives.

"My whole career was like that," Bobby said. "I had really, really good times, and I had disasters, where other people might have quit, but every time I hit a valley, I figured there had to be another hill out there."

For a man who has lost two sons, almost lost his own life, and lost his wife for a while, Bobby has lived life to the fullest. He smiles and tells his audiences, "I'm grateful."

STATISTICS

The following four races can be considered the backbone of the NASCAR tour. The Daytona 500 is the race with the most prize money, the Southern 500 is the oldest, the Talladega 500 is the fastest, and the World 600 is the longest.

DAYTONA 500

Year	Winner	Average Speed (mph)
1978	Bobby Allison	159.730
1982	Bobby Allison	153.991
1988	Bobby Allison	137.531
1992	Davey Allison	160.256

SOUTHERN 500

Year	Winner	Average Speed (mph)
1971	Bobby Allison	131.398
1972	Bobby Allison	128.124
1975	Bobby Allison	116.825
1983	Bobby Allison	123.343

TALLADEGA 500

Year	Winner	Average Speed (mph)
1971	Donnie Allison	145.945
1977	Donnie Allison	162.524

WORLD 600

Year	Winner	Average Speed (mph)
1970	Donnie Allison	129.680
1971	Bobby Allison	140.442
1981	Bobby Allison	129.326
1984	Bobby Allison	129.233
1991	Davey Allison	138.951

CAREER WINS

BOBBY ALLISON
Won more than $7.7 million in his career.

DONNIE ALLISON
Won more than 500 short track races.

DAVEY ALLISON
Won $6.7 million in his short career.

CHRONOLOGY

1959 Bobby and Donnie Allison leave Miami, Florida, in search of greater racing opportunities; they eventually settle in Hueytown, Alabama.

1965 After years of success in the modified circuit, Bobby decides to move up to the NASCAR Winston Cup Grand Nationals.

1966 Donnie follows in Bobby's footsteps, moving up to the Grand Nationals.

1971 In one of the most famous finishes in NASCAR history, Donnie edges out Bobby for a win at the Winston 500. Overall, 1971 is Bobby's year; he wins seven superspeedway races.

1978 After a major career slump that has lasted three seasons and during which he has not won for 67 races, Bobby makes a major comeback by winning the Daytona 500.

1979 Bobby's son Davey drives in his first major race, with an impressive fifth-place finish at Birmingham, Alabama.

1981 Donnie retires after sustaining massive head injuries in a crash at Charlotte, South Carolina.

1982 Bobby wins the Daytona 500 a second time, becoming only the third driver to win it more than once.

1983 After more than 20 years of racing and after losing by only a handful of points in 1981 and 1982, Bobby becomes the Winston Cup champion.

1987 Davey storms onto the NASCAR scene by qualifying for a first-row spot at the Daytona and is named Rookie of the Year.

1988 Bobby takes the Daytona 500 a third time, with Davey running a close second. Bobby is the oldest man ever to win a Winston Cup race. A few weeks later, major injuries sustained in a devastating crash at Pocono Raceway force Bobby to retire.

1992 Davey follows in his father's footsteps, winning the Daytona 500. Bobby's son Clifford is killed after crashing his car in a practice run in Michigan.

1993 Davey dies of major head injuries in a helicopter crash. Thousands of fans and members of the racing world mourn his loss.

1998 Bobby is inducted into the North Carolina Auto Racing Hall of Fame.

2003 The mayor of Hueytown, Alabama, declares the springtime Talladega race date as Davey Allison Day.

2005 Bobby is chosen to be honorary chairman and keynote speaker at the Tenth Annual Amelia Island Concourse d'Elegance classic car show in Florida. Bobby lobbies the state legislature of Florida to honor the memory of NASCAR greats with a new racing museum.

2006 The NASCAR Hall of Fame and Racing Museum is approved to be built in Charlotte, North Carolina. The Bobby Allison Grandstands are dedicated at Phoenix International Raceway. Bobby Allison narrates a NASCAR DVD board game and serves as spokesperson and guest commentator for a new reality TV show, *Reality Racing: The Rookie Challenge*. Kittie Allison, mother of Bobby and Donnie, is the guest of honor at a party to celebrate her one-hundredth birthday.

2007 Bobby and Judy's first great-grandchild, Allison Brooke Hinton, is born to Clifford's daughter and her husband.

GLOSSARY

drafting—When one car follows another very closely, and the front car pushes aside the air as it moves forward, a vacuum, or draft, is created between the rear end of the first car and the nose of the second car. The vacuum actually pulls the second car along, and that car is said to be "drafting".

flag—At the racetrack, flag colors have different meanings. Green: The race is started; Yellow: Caution, all drivers must slow down; Red: All drivers must stop; White: The lead car has one lap to go; Checkered: The winning car has crossed the finish line.

Grand Nationals—Since 1986, the official name of NASCAR's second highest level races.

NASCAR—National Association for Stock Car Racing, established in 1947, is the organizing group behind stock car racing; it makes and governs the rules for NASCAR racing.

pit stop—The time a car spends in its pit stall, an area designated for a team to service its cars. Racers want as short a pit stop as possible to get back into the race.

qualifying time—One at a time, race cars leave their pit stalls and, in less than one full lap, get up to speed. Drivers get the green flag as they cross the start/finish line to complete two laps. To set their best time, they choose the fastest of the two laps as their official qualifying time.

Rookie of the Year—NASCAR awards this honor to the first-year driver whose best 15 finishes are higher than any other first-year driver.

slingshotting—A move in which a car following the leader in a draft suddenly steers around the leader, breaking the vacuum and providing an extra burst of speed that allows the slingshotting can to take the lead.

stock car—An automobile that has not been modified from its original factory build, in contrast to a race car, which is a special, custom-built car designed for racing purposes only, with no intent of being used as regular transportation.

superspeedway—A racetrack of two miles or more in distance. Short tracks are less than one mile, intermediate tracks are at least one mile but less than two miles, and superspeedways are two miles or longer.

Victory Lane—A place on a racetrack where the winner parks after a race to be greeted by fans and receive a trophy. Sometimes called the "winner's circle."

Winston Cup—The highest level of NASCAR stock car racing, begun in 1949. Also known as NASCAR Cup or Sprint Cup, beginning in 2008.

BIBLIOGRAPHY

Allison, Bobby, and Tim Packman. *Bobby Allison: A Racer's Racer.* Champaign, Ill.: *Sports Publishing,* 2003.

"Bobby Allison: A Modern-Day Job." *Seattle Post-Intelligencer,* February 11, 1997.

Bolton, Clyde. *The Alabama Gang.* Birmingham, Ala.: Birmingham News, 1994.

Cutter, Robert, and Bob Fendell. *The Encyclopedia of Auto Racing Greats.* Englewood Cliffs, N.J.: Prentice Hall, Inc., 1973.

Golenbock, Peter. *Miracle: Bobby Allison and the Saga of the Alabama Gang.* New York: St. Martin's Press, 2006.

Griffin, Larry. "Sign of the Cross." *Car and Driver,* May 1990.

Grubba, Fr. Dale. *Testament of the Weekend Warrior.* Tucson, Ariz.: AZTEX Corporation, 1997.

Hinton, Ed. "How Much Can One Man Bear?" *Sports Illustrated,* February 10, 1997.

———. "The Fall of the House of Allison." *Car and Driver,* November 1993.

———. "Requiem for a Racing Man." *Sports Illustrated,* July 26, 1993.

Hunter, Don and Al Pearce. *The Illustrated History of Stock Car Racing.* Osceola, Wisc.: MBI Publishing Company, 1998.

Kreuzer, Laura. "After String of Tragedies, Bobby Allison is Back Where He Belongs." *Knight Ridder/Tribune News Service,* February 18, 1995.

McCarter, Mark. "The gang's not here." *The Sporting News,* March 25, 2002.

NASCAR.com. Available online. URL: *www.nascar.com* (accessed December 7, 2006).

Pimm, Nancy Roe. *Indy 500: The Inside Track.* Plain City, Ohio: Oxford Resources, Inc./Darby Creek Publishing, 2004.

FURTHER READING

Barber, Phil. *From Finish to Start: A Week in the Life of a NASCAR Racing Team*. Chanhassen, Minn.: Tradition Publishing Company, LLC/Tradition Books, 2004.

Bledsoe, Glen, and Karen Bledsoe. *The World's Fastest Indy Cars*. Minneapolis: Capstone Press Capstone High-Interest Books, 2003.

Brock, Ted. *The Busch Series: Shorter Races, Big Action*. Chanhassen, Minn.: Tradition Publishing Company, LLC/Tradition Books, 2004.

———. *Fast Families: Racing Together Through Life*. Chanhassen, Minn.: Tradition Publishing Company, LLC/Tradition Books, 2003.

Buckley, James, Jr.. *The Starting Line: Life as a NASCAR Rookie*. Chanhassen, Minn.: Tradition Publishing Company, LLC/ Tradition Books, 2004.

Cavin, Curt. *Race Day! The Fastest Show on Earth*. Chanhassen, Minn.: Tradition Publishing Company, LLC/Tradition Books, 2003.

———. *Terrific Tracks: The Coolest Places to Race*. Chanhassen, Minn.: Tradition Publishing Company, LLC/Tradition Books, 2004.

———. *Under the Helmet: Inside the Mind of a Driver*. Chanhassen, Minn.: Tradition Publishing Company, LLC/Tradition Books, 2004.

Cefrey, Holly. *Race Car Drivers: Life on the Fast Track*. New York: Rosen Publishing Group, Inc., 2001.

Edelstein, Robert. *NASCAR Generations: The Legacy of Family in NASCAR Racing*. New York: HarperCollins Publishers/ HarperEntertainment, 2000.

Fleischman, Bill, and Al Pearce. *The Unauthorized NASCAR Fan Guide 2004*. Detroit, Mich.: Visible Ink Press, 2004.

Gigliotti, Jim. *Fantastic Finishes: NASCAR's Great Races.* Chanhassen, Minn.: Tradition Publishing Company, LLC/ Tradition Books, 2004.

Johnstone, Michael. NASCAR: *The Need for Speed.* Minneapolis, Minn.: Lerner, 2002.

Martin, Mark. *NASCAR for Dummies.* New York: Wiley Publishing, Inc., 2000.

Menzer, Joe. *The Wildest Ride: A History of NASCAR (or How a Bunch of Good Ol' Boys Built a Billion-Dollar Industry out of Wrecking Cars).* New York: Simon & Schuster, 2001.

WEB SITES

www.belongshere.com
Information about the new NASCAR Hall of Fame in Charlotte, North Carolina.

www.bobbyallison.com
Bobby Allison's official Web site. Racing history, family history, his online store, and current events are updated regularly.

www.daytonausa.com/events
Daytona USA, "The Official Attraction of NASCAR", offers online videos of NASCAR racing, information, and event listings.

www.ihra.com
The Web site of IHRA Motorsports contains information about international hot rod racing.

www.msn.foxsports.com/nascar
Coverage of the NASCAR Nextel Cup includes results, schedules, standings, and more.

www.nascar.com
The official Web site for NASCAR information. This is the best place to start learning more about NASCAR. It has the latest results and driver standings as well as pages where readers can learn more about the sport in general.

www.nhra.com
NHRA: Championship Drag Racing tells about hot rod racing in the United States.

www.cascar.com
CASCAR Racing is the official Web site for Canadian racing information.

www.whowon.com
This site lists locations and results of races, posts racing schedules, and includes NASCAR information.

www.racingschools.com
The site advertises more than 70 auto-racing schools around the world.

www.sports.yahoo.com/nascar
The site covers NASCAR sports and provides fantasy auto racing, opinions and analysis from the pros, and pictures of the latest races.

www.1800bepetty.com
The Richard Petty Driving Experience Web site offers a celebrity gallery and an interactive drive-along experience.

PICTURE CREDITS

INDEX

A

Alabama Gang, 15, 34
Allison, Bobby
  birth, 9
  business side of racing, 11, 14,
    55, 57
  crashes, 8–10, 12, 14, 26, 31–34,
    44–46, 49, 51–52, 57–58
  crew, 7, 49
  designer and inventor, 28
  early racing years, 10–11, 18, 58
  fans, 15, 23, 26
  fines, 12
  feud with Petty, 24–26
  illnesses, 31–33, 35, 38
  injuries, 9, 12, 14, 31, 35, 51, 53–54,
    57–59, 62
  lectures, 12, 59
  modified racing, 18–22
  racing attitude, 9, 12–13, 23–24,
    31, 34, 58, 62
  retirement, 12–13, 49, 51–52
  rivalry with Donnie, 26–28, 30
  slumps, 31–34
  titles and honors, 30–31
  working on cars, 11–12, 19, 22, 28
Allison, Bonnie, 39
Allison, Carrie, 39
Allison, Clifford, 51, 57
  childhood, 7, 9, 39–41
  death, 14, 53–55, 58–59, 62
  early racing, 42, 52
  jockey, 7, 42
Allison, Davey, 51, 54, 57
  childhood, 7, 9, 39–41
  crashes, 44, 47, 52
  death, 14, 34, 54–56, 58–59, 62
  early racing, 42–46
  fans, 52, 55
  race with Bobby, 15–18, 44, 46, 49, 51
  reputation, 46–47
  titles and honors, 16, 44, 46, 48, 55

Allison, Donnie, 15, 43, 54
  crashes, 49, 57
  modified racing, 18–22, 58
  retirement, 49
  rivalry with Bobby, 26–28, 30
  titles and honors, 26–28
  working on cars, 19, 22
Allison, E.J., 15
Allison, Judy, 7, 39, 55, 58
  divorce, 59–60
  remarriage, 61–62
Allison, Kittie, 15
  faith, 53–54, 56–57
Allison Way, 14, 49, 57
  chronology, 65–66
  statistics, 63–64
Automobile Racing Club of American
  (ARCA), 44

B

Baker, Buddy, 9, 26, 30
Bobby Allison Motorsports, 14
Bonnett, Neil, 34
Bowman Gray Stadium, 23
Brooklyn, Michigan, 53
Bush Grand National series, 52–53

C

Carolina 500, 9, 31
Charlotte Motor Speedway, 27, 38, 49
Checkered flag, 18
Cruise, Tom, 17

D

Darlington, South Carolina, 44
Daytona 500, 36, 39
  Bobby and Dave race at, 15–18,
    44, 46, 51
  first race at, 12

history, 12, 17, 47–48
records at, 16
spectators at, 15
wins at, 7, 9, 15–16, 18, 24, 33–34,
    37–38, 48–49, 51, 55
Days of Thunder (movie), 17
DiGard/Gatorade team, 35
Dover, Delaware, 46
Drafting, 17–18, 36
Dukes of Hazard (television), 17

E

Earnhardt, Dale, 62
Elko, Minnesota
    crash at, 9, 31

G

Green flag, 17

H

Hialeah Speedway, 10
Hueytown, Alabama
    Allisons' hometown, 14–15, 21, 34,
        41, 44
Huntsville, Alabama, 12

I

Indianapolis 500, 27
Indianapolis Motor Speedway, 27
Indy racing
    rookies of the year, 27–28

J

Johnston, Junior, 44

L

Lilly, Betty, 22
London, New Hampshire, 55
"Luxury Liner," 7
    crashes with, 9, 31, 33–34

M

Marcis, Dave, 30
McReynolds, Larry, 46

Mercury Outboard, 11
Moonshine, 17
Moore, Bud, 33–34

N

NASCAR (National Association for
    Stock Car Auto Racing), 11, 42, 58
    drivers, 15
    Grand Nationals, 18, 22–23, 26,
        38, 44
    history, 17, 24, 28, 30–31
    officials, 12
    Rookies of the year, 16, 26, 46
    top honors, 31
National 500 (Charlotte Speedway)
    races at, 26–27

O

Olds, Ransom E., 12

P

Peach Fuzz Gang, 42
Petty, Adam, 60
Petty, Richard, 37, 60–61
    crashes, 26
    feud with Bobby, 24–26
    King Richard, 24
Pit stops, 9, 42
Pocono, Pennsylvania
    crashes at, 52, 54
Prohibition, 17

Q

Qualifying time, 7, 33

S

Slingshotting, 17–18, 36
Smokey and the Bandit (movie), 17
Sportsman Most Popular Driver honor, 28
Stock car racing, 11, 27
Super speedways, 15

T

Talladega, Alabama, 44–45
    crash at, 55

V

Victory Lane, 32, 46, 48

W

Waltrip, Darrell, 36
Winston 500, 28, 30
Winston Cup season
    races in, 16, 28, 35, 44, 46, 49, 55
    series champions, 24, 31, 36, 55

Winston-Salem, North Carolina, 23
World 600, 38
    wins at, 27

Y

Yarborough, Cale
    races against, 7, 9, 36–37

ABOUT THE AUTHOR

ANN PARR, a freelance writer and former elementary school teacher, lives with her husband in Lindsborg, Kansas, a quiet Swedish community. When she is not writing, she may be fulfilling business-consulting assignments with her husband, jogging, reading, playing the piano or organ, or visiting children and grandchildren. Parr recently completed her master's of fine arts degree in writing for children from Vermont College. She writes children's books and magazine articles, often about sports and sports figures.

Parr likes cars and remembers a time when she could identify the make and model of almost all the cars going up and down the highways. She also remembers learning to drive her dad's 1950 stick-shift, dead-green Chevrolet pickup truck. Parr says she appreciates how much race car drivers have to learn, practice, and give up in order to become great performers.